STEPS COURSE
ALONG THE PATHWAY TO THE SOUL

A guided practicum in Biblical, repeatable, and Spirit-led evangelism

Written and produced by
Church Partnership Evangelism

Copyright © 2019 by Church Partnership Evangelism
PO Box 5347, Boise, Idaho 83705 | www.traincpe.org

All rights reserved. No part of this material may be reproduced, scanned, or distributed in any printed or electronic form without permission.

Visit www.traincpe.org for access to a free and distributable electronic version of this course, as well as other supplemental materials.

First Edition: November 2019
ISBN: 978-1-70035-431-0

Unless otherwise noted, all Scripture quotations are taken from the ESV® Bible, copyright © 2001 by Crossway, a publishing ministry of Good News Publishers. Used by permission. All rights reserved.

Consider supporting the work of Church Partnership Evangelism at www.traincpe.org/give

Church Partnership Evangelism (CPE) exists as a resource of training and guidance to the local church and its leaders for the sole purpose of building up the kingdom and body of Christ. CPE is committed to equipping, encouraging, and engaging every believer in personal evangelism, personal discipleship, and the planting of new churches.

Our desire is to make disciples and to make disciples into disciple-makers. This is accomplished through the faithful proclamation of the life, death, and resurrection of our Lord Jesus.

to equip the saints for the work of ministry, for building up the body of Christ.

Ephesians 4:12

Additional resources provided by CPE
and made available at www.traincpe.org:

Pathway to the Soul
Reaching People
Through Spirit-led Dialogue

**Essential Truths
of the Christian Life**
A 17-lesson resource
for personal discipleship

Saving Evangelicals
A discipleship resource to
help you assess your own
testimony of salvation.

Contents

Course Introduction 1

Step 1: We Are Intercessors 7

Step 2: Pray with Burdens for People and Passions for God 13

Step 3: Listen to What God is Saying to Lost People 21

Step 4: Know Your Story of Salvation 29

Step 5: Discover What People Know About God and About Their Sin 37

Step 6: Bring People Before the Cross and to The Door of Their Hearts 45

Step 7: Disciple the New Christian 53

Step 8. Be Filled with the Holy Spirit 63

Step 9: Go Dialogue with Them the Good News 71

Appendix A: Prayer Covenant 77
Appendix B: Suggested Dialogue Questions 78
Appendix C: 10 Questions 83

Course Introduction

PREPARING TO GO!
We are not here because we simply want to learn about evangelism. We are taking this course so that we can do evangelism. We want to persuade lost people to put saving faith in the Savior Jesus Christ. This means we must commit to go when the time comes. And we must be willing to speak when the opportunity is presented. And while our aim is to persuade, we understand that God has called us to be obedient, not successful.

COVERED IN PRAYER
The work ahead—the evangelization and discipleship of new believers in your community—is a work that depends entirely on the Holy Spirit. Only He can prepare hearts, reveal truth, and empower your witness. Be sure to submit this course, every meeting, and every participant, to God through deep and thoughtful prayer. This course will regularly encourage times of prayer. When time is limited, prayer seems to be the first thing that is set aside for the sake of getting through more material. *Do not allow this to happen.* Remain committed to seeking the Lord in prayer at every turn. Constant prayer will help maintain a spirit of humility and dependence on God, and it will build in you a confidence in the power of the Holy Spirit to do the work of convicting and saving souls.

FOR NON-EVANGELISTS
Not everyone has the supernatural gift of faith, giving, mercy, service, or hospitality. But God expects us to learn from and even imitate those who do. Many of us may not have the supernatural gift of evangelism, but we are all here to be inspired and equipped for the task together. In fact, while we likely have many different spiritual gifts, it is what we have in common that brings us together. We have a common testimony of salvation and we have the same Holy Spirit empowering our witness. And so, we are compelled to the same work.

A HOLY AMBITION
Everyone desires to do great things. Daniel 12:3 says that those who lead many to righteousness will shine like the stars! Jesus, when His disciples were arguing over who would be the greatest in the kingdom, did not rebuke them for their ambition. Instead, he directed it (Luke 22:24-30). We are taking this class because we desire to do great things *for God!* And nothing is greater than sharing with others the hope of eternal life through Jesus Christ.

MORE READY THAN WE KNOW
The joyful work of evangelism is not beyond us. Our desire to share Christ's Gospel comes from God. The same God who placed in our hearts the desire to share His

good news will prepare hearts to receive that good news. God prepares us to share the Gospel with those He prepares to hear it. *Both are more ready than we know!*

INTERCEDE – INVITE – INSTRUCT

The work before us will follow three key movements. In the first movement, through lessons 1-3, we will explore our role as *intercessors*. In the second movement, through lessons 4-6, we will add to this role an understanding of dialogue evangelism that results in an *invitation* to receive the gift of Jesus Christ. In the final movement, through lessons 7-9, we will add to these a commitment to go and make disciples (rather than simply converts) by *instructing* them in the ways and commands of Jesus.

STRUCTURE

This course has a distinct structure to it. There are 9 lessons to be unpacked over 9 weekly meetings. Each lesson builds on the truths explored in the previous lesson. Therefore, it is important that each step is covered, and none are skipped. It is recommended that the following steps are covered one week at a time in a small group study. Because of the importance of each step, each participant should commit to full participation and to carrying out the assignments given at the end of each step.

FIRST THINGS: THE GOSPEL

All people were created in God's image, to reflect His glory and enjoy Him in intimate relationship. All people have sinned and fall short of God's glory, are thus separated from God, and have earned physical, spiritual, and eternal death as a just punishment. Man is unable to save himself, meaning there is nothing he can do to avoid the penalty of death or to earn salvation by any amount of good works or religion. Instead, Jesus, who is fully God and fully man, lived a sinless life, died on a cross in our place, satisfying the penalty of death that we could not avoid, and rose from the dead three days later winning for us the life we could never earn. Man is saved from sin's penalty, given Christ's righteousness and eternal life, and reconciled to God as a gift of God's grace alone, accomplished by Christ's death and resurrection, to be received by personal repentance and faith in the Lord Jesus Christ.

> The message of who Jesus is and what He has done, is The Gospel, and it is "the power of God for salvation to everyone who believes." Romans 1:16

COURSE OUTLINE

STEP 1: WE ARE INTERCESSORS
If people who do not know Jesus as their Savior think of you as their *evangelist* (if they think you are going to preach at them) they will often avoid you. If they think of you as their *intercessor* (if they think you are going to pray for them) they will often seek you out. We will explore this identity in Step 1.

STEP 2: PRAY WITH BURDENS FOR PEOPLE AND PASSIONS FOR GOD
If we are to approach evangelism correctly, we must do so as intercessors. This is our reason for relationships with unbelievers and why we are called to personal evangelism. We are to see ourselves as their intercessors. Our evangelism needs to begin with prayer. This is not just any kind of prayer, but deep, intentional prayer produced in us by the Holy Spirit. It is this high place that we must commit ourselves to journeying to.

STEP 3: LISTEN TO WHAT GOD IS SAYING TO LOST PEOPLE
Having committed to a specific time of intercession for members of your unbelieving *oikos*, it is important for you to know that the Holy Spirit is already at work in their lives. He is conducting a conversation with them into which we should learn to listen. What are the things we should expect that the Holy Spirit will be saying to them? What points of conversation should we be listening for?

STEP 4: KNOW YOUR STORY OF SALVATION
If you have indeed been rescued by God's grace through Jesus Christ, then you possess a testimony that is powerful to draw lost people into a realization of their own sin and need for a Savior. There may be nothing more natural to a conversation with lost people than to share your own discovery of the Savior and to invite them to "Come and see." John 1:46

STEP 5: DISCOVER WHAT PEOPLE KNOW ABOUT GOD AND ABOUT THEIR SIN
After a period of dedicated intercession for the lost people in our *oikos*, there is a need to move intentionally into gracious dialogue with each person. This will be a conversation where we listen for the evidence of God's preparing grace and we share the message of God's saving grace. Now that we are armed with the gospel and the story of our salvation, we are compelled by Christ to actively pursue opportunities to speak of these things with lost people.

STEP 6: BRING PEOPLE TO THE CROSS AND TO THE DOOR OF THEIR HEARTS
We are anticipating a conversation with those who have been the subject of our ongoing intercession. By the leading of the Holy Spirit the first part of our conversation will put them before God and their own sins. Now let us consider how to lead them to the cross where Christ died for them and before a door where Christ is knocking.

STEP 7: DISCIPLE THE NEW CHRISTIAN
God calls us to make disciples, not lead people to make decisions. Our work is not done when people pray to receive Jesus as their savior. Now we must intentionally join our evangelism with the ongoing work of personal discipleship. The conversation that the Holy Spirit is having with each person continues after they believe in Christ as their Savior and surrender to Him as Lord. So, our role and our opportunity to join that conversation continues as well.

STEP 8: BE FILLED WITH THE HOLY SPIRIT
The truth is that much of what we have learned could be practiced by a Christian as an exercise of their own effort. That Christian's evangelism may look and feel like real and genuine evangelism, but it is wholly inadequate so long as is it is not compelled and propelled by the Spirit of God in them. The Holy Spirit is ready to fill us and we should not take another step in the way of evangelism without the filling of the Holy Spirit who goes with us and goes before us.

STEP 9: GO DIALOGUE WITH THEM THE GOOD NEWS
Today we begin a two-week period of intense personal evangelism and discipleship. Our time of intercession for those in our *oikos* and our training together has brought us to this time of action. Our intercession is about to reach its climax as we present to our lost friends and family members the *ultimate intercessor*, our Lord Jesus Christ.

1

He saw that there was no man, and wondered that there was no one to intercede; then his own arm brought him salvation, and his righteousness upheld him.

Isaiah 59:16

Step 1: We Are Intercessors

NOTES

INTRODUCTION TO STEP 1
If people who do not know Jesus as their Savior think of you as their *evangelist* (if they think you are going to preach at them) they will often avoid you. If they think of you as their *intercessor* (if they think you are going to pray for them) they will often seek you out. We will explore this identity in Step 1.

LEARNING OBJECTIVES
We will learn the importance of being recognized by others as an intercessor. We will learn the biblical basis for our role as intercessors. We will learn what an intercessor is and what an intercessor does. And we will consider who should be the focus of our intercession.

BE AN INTERCESSOR BEFORE YOU ARE AN EVANGELIST
Our primary identity before others is not that of an evangelist. If we primarily think of ourselves as evangelists, we will find it increasingly difficult to succeed in evangelism.

1. **An *intercessor* is someone who:**

   - Represents people to God. 1 Timothy 2:1–4
   - Represents God to people. 2 Corinthians 5:20
   - Turns the focus on God and on others. The focus is not on us. John 3:30
   - Our Lord Jesus did this perfectly on the cross.

     Question: In what way did Christ represent *us* to *God* on the cross?

     Question: In what way did Christ represent *God* to *us* on the cross?

2. **An *intercessor* must know both God and people.**
   Because of this, we should walk a well-worn path between God and people. We must spend time getting to know the

God *to* whom we intercede, and we must spend time getting to know the people *for* whom we intercede.

- Moses walked the path of intercession. Exodus 33:7–11
- Our Lord Jesus walked the path of intercession during his earthly ministry. Mark 1:29-39
- The climax of Christ's intercessory work took place on the cross.

> **Question:** Like Moses, how might people watch you more closely if they knew you were praying for them? What will they see? What will they think?

3. **An intercessor answers a Biblical calling.**

- The Bible teaches that we are to become more and more like Christ who "lives to make intercession." Hebrews 7:25
- We will not fully understand Christ's intercession for sinners and for us, until we do the work of intercession ourselves.

4. **An intercessor embraces three realities.**

- *Identification.* Jesus identified with us by becoming like us. An intercessor identifies deeply with those for whom he intercedes. He does his very best to not only understand their circumstances but to identify with them. We know the sin that enslaves them (Romans 3:23). Likewise, we know the grace that has saved us and can alone save them (Titus 2:11).

- *Agony.* Jesus agonized for us. Romans 8:26 teaches that even now the Holy Spirit "intercedes for us with groanings too deep for words." The same Holy Spirit dwells in us. Our identification is incomplete if we do not agonize over the sins, burdens, and sufferings of those for whom we intercede.

- *Authority.* Jesus' intercession worked for us by turning away God's wrath! Our intercession is not a substitute for sin as it is in Jesus, but our identification and agony on behalf of others *works.* God responds (Genesis 19:29).

    Question: What might it look like for us to become weak, that we might win the weak, as Paul claims to do in 1 Corinthians 9:19-23?

    Question: What does Paul's statement in Romans 9:3 say about his agony for Israelites?

    Question: Can we expect our intercession to work? Why?

    Question: Can you identify these three realities of Christ's intercession (identification, agony, authority) in Philippians 2:5-11?

5. **An *intercessor* leaves an impression.**
   The Lord was called a "friend of sinners" (Matthew 11:19). Those with him realized two things.

- "He is our friend."
- "and we are sinners."
- Read John 8:3-11 and answer the following questions.

    Question: How did Jesus make the woman feel like He was her *friend?*

    Question: How did Jesus make the woman feel like she was a sinner?

Our lives of intercession before others should leave them with the impression that we care for them as our friends and at the same time remain different from them in a way that quietly convicts them of their sinful spiritual condition.

NOTES

NOTES

Now the question is ... who should be the primary focus of our intercession?

THE *OIKOS* PRINCIPLE OF EVANGELISM

We should intercede for our *oikos*. The Greek word *oikos* referred to an individual's home. It also often referred to those living as a part of the economy of that home (slaves, servants, children, relatives, friends, and acquaintances). The basic thrust of evangelism in the New Testament has been called "*oikos* evangelism." *Oikos* evangelism builds on the natural webs of relationship within families, communities, or common interests.

1. ***Oikos* evangelism from the Gospels.**

   - Mark 5:14–20: "Go home to your friends" (v. 19).
   - Luke 19:1–10: "Today salvation has come to this house," (v. 9).
   - Mark 2:14–15: "And as he reclined at the table in his [Levi's] house, many tax collectors and sinners were reclining with Jesus…for there were many who followed him." (v. 15).

2. ***Oikos* evangelism in the book of Acts.**

   - Acts 10:1–2, 22–24: Who heard the good news of Christ with Cornelius?
   - Acts 16:11–15: "after she was baptized, and her household as well,"
   - Acts 16:25–34: "They answered, 'Believe in the Lord Jesus, and you will be saved, you and your household,'" (v. 31).

3. **Identify your *oikos*.**

   - We may know hundreds of people, but we have very few close, meaningful relationships.
   - These are our *oikos* and therefore the key focus of our intercession and the primary target of our evangelism.

ASSIGNMENT

- Identify the unbelievers in your *oikos* whom you want to see come to Christ, including friends, family, fellow workmates, neighbors, and others within the circle of your domestic life (i.e., service providers).
- Make a list of these names (approx. 4-8) and bring them with you to our next time of training.
- Read Jeremiah chapter 14

NOTES

> "I am an intercessor. I represent God to people and people to God. Therefore, I must take time to know God and take time to know people."

2

"Now therefore let me alone, that my wrath may burn hot against them and I may consume them, in order that I may make a great nation of you." But Moses implored the Lord his God...

Exodus 32:10-11a

Step 2: Pray with Burdens for People and Passions for God

NOTES

REVIEW OF STEP 1
We learned that our most important identity before others is that of an intercessor. We learned that an intercessor is one who stands between God and people, representing both to the other. We learned that an intercessor knows the realities of *identification, agony,* and *authority,* based on the example of Christ's intercession for us. And we learned that our primary work of intercession should be focused on our *oikos,* or those who make up the natural web of relationships we share with our families and communities.

LAST WEEK'S ASSIGNMENT
Take time for each participant to stand and read their list of unbelieving *oikos* names aloud. Once they finish, have them declare out loud, before the group, "This is my *oikos*, and I am their intercessor." Have someone record all the names that are read and consider posting the list of names somewhere for all participants to see throughout the time of training. In the following weeks, you will take time to pray together over these names when you meet.

INTRODUCTION TO STEP 2
If we are to approach evangelism correctly, we must do so as intercessors. This is our reason for relationships with unbelievers and why we are called to personal evangelism. We are to see ourselves as their intercessors. Our evangelism needs to begin with prayer. This is not just any kind of prayer, but deep, intentional prayer produced in us by the Holy Spirit. It is this high place that we must commit ourselves to journeying to.

LEARNING OBJECTIVES
We will learn that reaching the high place of intercession takes time and effort. We will understand what motivates our intercession. Taken from Jeremiah 14, we will learn what burdens and prayers a life of intercession will produce. We will learn that intercession is the place where our passion for people intersects with our passion for God.

NOTES

INTERCESSION TAKES TIME AND EFFORT

God called Moses to intercede for the people of Israel. God said to Moses, "Be ready ... come up ... present yourself there to me on the top of the mountain" (Exodus 34:2). There is no such thing as an easy intercession. Like Moses, we must also be willing to climb a mountain.

> Turn to Jeremiah 14 to discover how the place of intercession is reached when our passion for people and our passion for God intersect in our hearts by the power of the Holy Spirit.

FOUR BURDENS FOR PEOPLE

Our intercession will grow in its impact as we learn to pray for people in four ways. Ask God to cultivate in you these burdens for lost people.

1. **Be burdened for the *sins* of others.** Jeremiah was burdened by the people's sin.

   - He does not say, "*They* have sinned" but "*We* have sinned," and "*Our* iniquities testify against us." Jeremiah 14:7 & 20
   - Jesus is our perfect example. He knows the full weight of sin's temptation and fully identifies with our sins. Hebrews 4:15, 2 Corinthians 5:21

     Question: What are some sins that have a hold on those you know who are lost?

     Question: How do you react to the sins of others? How would you react as an intercessor?

2. **Be burdened by the judgment sin requires.** Jeremiah was burdened by the consequences of their sin.

   - He sees and is burdened by the wrath and rejection of God that is to come because of the people's sin, even if they did not see it themselves. Jeremiah 14:8b & 19

- A godly parent intercedes for a child who does not know the consequences of the sin they are enjoying. But the parent knows the consequence and weeps.
- Jesus knows the destruction that sin produces in our lives. Luke 19:41-44, Galatians 6:8

    Question: What negative consequences do sins produce in the lives of those you know?

    Question: Have you felt this burden for someone? Can you describe that feeling?

3. **Be burdened for the *needs* of others.** In Jeremiah 14:7, Jeremiah prays for rain. His request is simply, "Act, O Lord!" This cry for action is a call for God to meet the immediate needs of the people during physical drought and famine.

- Always consider the spiritual issues to be central to a person's deepest needs.
- But do not forget the basic needs of that person's life as well.
- Again, Jesus is our perfect example, whose ministry is one of constantly meeting people's basic needs.

    Question: What are some basic needs that we can be aware of and praying for in the lives of others?

4. **Be burdened even to *defend* others.** Jeremiah was moved to speak in their defense.

- Jeremiah's defense is imperfect, but his passion for the people he prays for causes him to speak up to defend them before God. Jeremiah 14:13-16
- A mother prays, "It is not my son, it is his friends."
- Jesus defended those who nailed Him to the cross. Luke 23:34

    Question: What are some influences that lead people to sin that you can identify with?

NOTES

> We are moved by their **sins**, by the **judgment** their sin requires, by their basic **needs**, and by the desire to speak in their **defense**. Only the Holy Spirit, sent from Christ, possesses these burdens, and can work them into the heart of an intercessor.

FOUR PASSIONS FOR GOD

We will come into intercession as our prayers reflect a passion for God in four ways. We are truly interceding when these passions for God combine with our burdens for people. Read Jeremiah 14:21–22 and identify the following passions for God.

1. **Be passionate for *God's name*.**

   o "Do not spurn us, for *Your name's sake*."
   o This is a passion that God's attributes would be shown and known.

   > **Question:** What are some of God's attributes that you want people to understand?

2. **Be passionate for *God's glory*.**

   o "Do not disgrace the throne of *Your glory*."
   o This is a passion that God's presence would be felt.

   > **Question:** What would be their reaction if those you prayed for became aware of God's presence?

3. **Be passionate for *God's Word*.**

   o "Do not break your covenant with us."
   o This is a passion that God's promises would prevail.

   > **Question:** What promises of God do you want the people you are praying for to receive?

4. **Be passionate for *God's fame*.**

   o   "Are there any among the false idols of the nations that can bring rain? Or can the heavens give showers? *Are you not he, O LORD our God?*"
   o   This is a passion that God would be exalted in praise above all else.

   > **Question**: What idols in your culture does God's fame need to rise above?

We reach the high ground of intercession when our burden for others and our passion for God unites in our hearts. As we pray, God is preparing the soil of their hearts for His Word. At the same time, He begins preparing someone to sow the seed. We may find that the sower He is preparing is us (Luke 10:1–3). Arriving at this true intercession will be demonstrated by our willingness to be an answer for the very things for which we are praying.

APPLICATION: MAKE A "PRAYER COVENANT" WITH GOD

If we want to bring people to Jesus, we must commit ourselves to interceding for them with deep and intentional prayer. This kind of prayer can only be cultivated in us by the Holy Spirit. We must commit ourselves to interceding for our lost friends, family members, neighbors, and fellow workers. *God will guide us in these prayers.* We must also be prepared for an investment of time and effort in order to reach the place of intercession. Let us commit ourselves to interceding for our *oikos*.

1. **Ask God to give you these four burdens and passions.**

2. **Ask God to give you opportunities to display these burdens and passions in your actions.**
   The love of God draws men to Himself (Jeremiah 31:3). Ask God to reveal to you how you can show the love of Jesus to the people you are praying for. Whatever God shows you, *obey him*. He is answering your prayer.

NOTES

3. ***IMPORTANT: Tell them you are praying for them.**
   You are to tell these people about your commitment to pray for them. Tell them that you will be praying that the Creator God would bless their life. Tell them that you will pray every day for a specific period. Ask them what needs you can pray for. Now they will see themselves as someone who is being prayed for and they will see you as one who is praying for them.

4. **Here is the promise we will make.**
   We will pledge to pray faithfully for specific friends, family members, neighbors, and workmates every day for 60 to 90 days.

Almighty God,

I know that You desire for those I know and love to come to You in faith and find salvation through Your Son Jesus Christ. I know that You long to forgive them of their sins and put in them Your eternal life. I now pledge to seek Your desire for these individuals in my prayers and actions.

I pledge for the next ___ months to pray every day, making specific requests on behalf of... (list names below)
Friends _____
Family members _____
Workmates _____
Neighbors _____

I pledge to seek Your Holy Spirit to guide me in my prayers for them. I ask that You use this time of intercession to prepare their hearts for the new life You wish to give them through Your Son.

*In Jesus' name, amen.   (sign your name)*_____

ASSIGNMENT   NOTES

- Complete the above prayer covenant.
- During the week, go directly to those you have pledged to pray for and tell them of your commitment to pray for them daily for a specified period.
- Collect prayer requests from them and be ready to share about these conversations during our next meeting.

"I am an intercessor. I represent God to people and people to God. Therefore, I must take time to know God and take time to know people."

3

But I ask, have they not heard? Indeed they have, for "Their voice has gone out to all the earth, and their words to the ends of the world."

Romans 10:18

Step 3: Listen to What God Is Saying to Lost People

NOTES

REVIEW OF STEP 2
We learned that as intercessors, our first step in personal evangelism begins with a commitment to prayer. We learned that reaching the high ground of intercession takes an investment of time and effort and will occur when our burden for people combines with our passion for God. We learned that our prayers should reflect a burden for people's sins, for the judgment their sin requires, for their immediate needs, and to the point of even defending them before God. We learned that our prayers should also reflect a passion for God's name, God's glory, God's word, and God's fame. True intercession prepares the soil for the seed of the Gospel and prepares the sowers who will cast that seed.

LAST WEEK'S ASSIGNMENT
The members of the class were instructed to approach those they have committed to praying for and tell them that they have pledged to pray for them every day for the next 60 to 90 days. Have each member of the class stand and give a report on his or her experience. *What were the reactions of those whom they approached? What were some of the prayer requests that they received?* In a large class, members should separate into smaller groups of three or four. Finish this time by praying together as a group over these individuals.

INTRODUCTION TO STEP 3
Having committed to a specific time of intercession for members of your unbelieving *oikos,* it is important for you to know that the Holy Spirit is already at work in their lives. He is conducting a conversation with them into which we should learn to listen. What are the things we should expect that the Holy Spirit will be saying to them? What points of conversation should we be listening for?

LEARNING OBJECTIVES
From John 16:8-11, we will learn that the Holy Spirit convicts all people (1) of their own sin, (2) of their need to be righteous and

NOTES

their lack of righteousness, and (3) of the prospect of oncoming judgment. We will learn how we can join the conversation the Holy Spirit is *already having* with the unbeliever. We will learn to listen for evidence of God's **convicting grace** in the lives of the lost. In this way, we will gain confidence to speak to that conviction, in a gracious and powerful manner, about God's **saving grace** through Jesus Christ.

> **Read John 16:8-11:** And when he comes, he will convict the world concerning sin and righteousness and judgment: concerning sin, because they do not believe in me; concerning righteousness, because I go to the Father, and you will see me no longer; concerning judgment, because the ruler of this world is judged.

THREE POINTS OF CONVICTION

Sin, *righteousness*, and *judgment* are the subjects of conversation that the Holy Spirit is most concerned with in all people. Note how Jesus says that this conviction will begin when the Holy Spirit is sent to us at Pentecost. What does that mean for the work of the Holy Spirit prior to Pentecost?

> **Question:** In the history of the human race, when was the first time that the Holy Spirit convicted a person of sin and righteousness and judgment?

THE HOLY SPIRIT HAS ALWAYS CONVICTED OF SIN, RIGHTEOUSNESS, AND JUDGMENT

Read Genesis 3:7-11

1. **Adam knew his sin.**
   He knew he was naked and exposed.

2. **Adam knew his need to be righteous.**
   Adam's covering of fig leaves was the first man-made religion. It was an attempt to cover his sin and hide his condition.

3. **Adam feared judgment.**
   Adam knew his covering was not sufficient to hide his sin and was afraid of God's reaction to his naked condition, so he hid himself.

A GREATER CONVICTING WORK BEGAN AT PENTECOST
John 16:8-11 teaches of the added power to convict people that the Holy Spirit would express when He came and filled the Christian with Jesus' presence and used them to tell others about Jesus' saving work. The presence of Jesus Christ brings the greatest depth of conviction.

1. **The conviction of sin, righteousness, and judgment did not change.**
   It is the same conviction experienced by Adam in the garden.

2. **The Holy Spirit at Pentecost added a new way of conviction.**
   Pentecost put the presence of Jesus Christ, with power, into the heart of every believer. The Holy Spirit now places Jesus Christ before lost people through an internally transformed community of Christians and their transforming message of the gospel.

3. **This is the Holy Spirit's *final* convicting work.**
   There will be no greater revealing of Christ's presence, until He comes in judgment.

4. **This is the Holy Spirit's greatest convicting work.**
   The full power of the Spirit's conviction occurs when our witness (of Christ and His gospel) meets with the already active and internal conviction of the Spirit in a person's life.

NOTES

NOTES

> The age long convicting work of the Holy Spirit is an act of **common grace** that prepares an unbeliever for the message of the gospel. The Christian intensifies the Spirit's convicting work by proclaiming, through the power of the Holy Spirit, the **saving grace** found in the person and work of Jesus Christ. Therefore, evangelism is a dialogue between one person, who is under the **convicting grace** of God, and another person who has experienced the **saving grace** of God.

OBSERVATION: TWO SPIRITUAL REALITIES DISCOVERED IN EVERY PLACE

Because God created all people to worship the Creator, every person is religious, and cannot help but worship. Read Acts 17:22 and Romans 1:22-23.

1. **Reality #1: God has put "eternity into man's hearts."**
   Ecclesiastes 3:11

   o By convicting all of sin, righteousness, and judgment.
   o Through the implanted image of God in all people.
   o Therefore, every man has a desire for what is transcendent and is interested in eternity.

2. **Reality #2: Man will not seek God for the answers.**
   Romans 3:11

   o Man will not go to God in response to His convicting work.
   o Man, instead, suppresses the work of God in their lives. Romans 1:18

3. **Result: Every false religion.**
   These two realities meet to produce all manner of false faiths. But beneath every false faith is still the good work of the Holy Spirit. Observe how every religion tries to address the same three convictions.

- Every religion seeks to limit the impact of man's **sin.**
- Every religion has a strategy for producing **righteousness.**
- Every religion proposes to avoid or mitigate **judgment.**

4. **Our response.**

- We do not need to engage people in religious debates and arguments.
- We do not have to confront the falseness of their worship.
- We can instead talk with them about their impulse to worship in the first place.
- We can instead address every man's awareness of their sin, their desire to be "good," and their fear of judgment.
- This is where a gentle conversation could be the most convicting and impactful. 2 Timothy 2:24-26

APPLICATION: WHAT DOES THIS MEAN FOR OUR WITNESS?

An understanding of the Holy Spirit's conviction ahead of us should shape the way we approach the work of intercession and evangelism.

1. **The Holy Spirit is working ahead of us, and always has been.**

   When we recognize this truth, we find the *key* to reaching *any* individual, in *any* culture, in *any* religion, and in *any* place. In fact, we can be confident that we will never begin a conversation with someone about Jesus that the Holy Spirit has not already begun.

2. **The Holy Spirit's work of conviction is not complete without us.**

   This does not mean that God *needs* us. According to His sovereign will and pleasure, God has determined to bring His full convicting work to the world through us, and by no other means. We bring to convicted people the Spirit's best and final argument through our faithful witness of Christ.

NOTES

3. **Let them speak.**
   If the Spirit is working ahead of us in the lives of unbelievers, then they have something to tell us. And we must listen.

4. **Listen sincerely for the evidence of the Spirit's work in the lives of lost people.**
   When unbelievers speak about their sin, their desire to be good, and their fear of judgment, they are revealing the work of the Holy Spirit. We must help people talk about these things and listen to them as they do. This is evidence of the grace of God preparing them for the gospel.

5. **Prepare to speak gently and directly.**
   The pathway into a person's soul is a conversation—one that the Holy Spirit has already begun. As people speak of their sin, their desire to be good, and their fear of judgment, by their own words they are opening themselves up to the familiar echoes of the Spirit in the gospel of Jesus Christ.

If God is already speaking by the Spirit to the hearts of people, then the most important words they can hear when coming to Christ, are **not our words but theirs** as they expose the convicting work of the Spirit in their own life.

ASSIGNMENT

- Pair up with a prayer partner with the assignment of meeting together once a week for the remainder of the course to pray through each other's *oikos* list.
- Memorize the Ten Commandments. Exodus 20:1–17
- Write a statement about which of the 10 Commandments God used to convince you of your sin and need for salvation.

~

> *"I am an intercessor. I represent God to people and people to God. Therefore, I must take time to know God and take time to know people. I know that the Holy Spirit works ahead of me speaking into the lives of unbelievers."*

4

For you have heard of my former life in Judaism, how I persecuted the church of God violently and tried to destroy it.

Galatians 1:13

Step 4: Know Your Story of Salvation

NOTES

REVIEW OF STEP 3
We learned that the Holy Spirit goes ahead of us, speaking into the lives of all people and preparing them for the Gospel. We learned from John 16:8–11 that the Spirit's ongoing work is to convict people of their sin, their need to be righteous, and the prospect of oncoming judgment. We learned that this convicting conversation that the Holy Spirit is already having with all people is a conversation that God invites us to join. We learned that we must help unbelievers speak of the conviction that the Spirit is conducting in their lives, and that as we listen sincerely, we position ourselves to speak to that conviction with God's saving grace through Jesus Christ.

LAST WEEK'S ASSIGNMENT
Confirm that each student remains committed to meeting at least once a week with their prayer partner for the remainder of the course to pray through one another's *oikos* list. Have all the students attempt, either together or in small groups, to recite the Ten Commandments. Then, in smaller groups, have each individual share how God used one of these commandments to convict them of their own sinfulness.

INTRODUCTION TO STEP 4
If you have indeed been rescued by God's grace through Jesus Christ, then you possess a testimony that is powerfully equipped to draw lost people into a realization of their own sin and need for a Savior. There may be nothing more natural to a conversation with lost people than to share your own discovery of the Savior and to invite them to "Come and see." John 1:46

LEARNING OBJECTIVES
We will learn to express our own story of salvation. Using Paul's testimony in Acts 26, we will learn a helpful outline for telling our stories of salvation. We will learn what kind of impression a genuine story of salvation should leave on others. We will also learn six important experiences that should be part of every true Christian's salvation story.

NOTES

THE GREATEST TRAGEDY

John 15:26–27 says, "But when the Helper comes ... he will bear witness about me. And you also will bear witness, because you have been with me from the beginning." This means that we cannot bear witness to what we have not experienced for ourselves.

- It is possible not to be confident of your salvation. This is a great tragedy. 1 John 5:13
- It is also possible to be confident of a salvation you do not possess. This is the *greatest* tragedy. Matthew 7:22-23
- To avoid these two tragedies, we must know our story and test it. 2 Corinthians 13:5

HOW TO OUTLINE YOUR STORY

Read Paul's testimony before Festus and King Agrippa in Acts 26:1–29. While you read, identify the following outline and begin thinking about the same parts of your own story of salvation.

1. **My life before coming to Christ. Acts 26:1–11**
2. **The events that brought me to Christ. Acts 26:12–18**
3. **How I turned to Christ. Acts 26:12-18**
4. **My life since choosing to follow Christ. Acts-26:19-23**

HOW WILL LOST PEOPLE RESPOND TO A STORY OF TRUE SALVATION?

An unbeliever's response to a genuine story of salvation will be drastic. To a heart not yet softened by the Holy Spirit, your story of salvation may sound crazy. To a heart that has been prepared by the Holy Spirit, your story of salvation may be persuasive.

- Festus said, "Paul, you are out of your mind." Acts 26:24
- Agrippa said, "In a short time would you persuade me to be a Christian?" Acts 26:28

NOTES

> The unbeliever's response to a genuine testimony of salvation will probably be twofold. He may think, *"You are crazy!"* But then he may think, *"There might be something to this!"*

TEST YOUR STORY FOR THE SIX ESSENTIAL EXPERIENCES OF SALVATION

To produce this reaction, our testimony should include the six essential experiences of salvation. These six things also prove the reality of the saving work of Jesus Christ that grants us eternal life.

1. **We were awakened.** Ephesians 5:14
   The first thing God does in rescuing you is that He awakens you to the need for rescue.

   A realization that you are not equipped to face the momentary challenges of life is not the same as that awakening where you realize the desperate condition of not having an answer for life at all. Acts 2:37

   > **Question:** Can you recall when you experienced ineffectual awakenings? How did you respond? How was this different from times of true awakening from God?

2. **We repented.** Mark 1:14–15
   True repentance is a radical change of mind that turns you from your normal pattern of defending yourself.

   o   Repentance is not equal to remorse, regret, shame, or simply saying "I'm sorry."
   o   Repentance is when you accept God's argument against you, that you are a sinner (Romans 3:23), that because of your sins you deserve hell (Romans 6:23a), that your good works are stained and worthless (Isaiah 64:6), and that by ruling your own life you rebel against God.

NOTES

Question: Can you recall times of false repentance when you did not turn fully from yourself, your sin, your self-righteousness, and your self-rule? What did that false repentance look and feel like? How did the moment of true repentance differ from those other occasions?

3. **We exercised saving faith.** Ephesians 2:8–9
   Saving faith follows true repentance when your mind takes up God's argument *for* you!

   o The Lord Jesus is your sinless representative. 2 Corinthians 5:21
   o The Lord Jesus suffered on the cross and took your punishment in your place. Romans 3:24-25
   o The Lord Jesus covers you with His perfect righteousness. Romans 13:14
   o You bow to Jesus as Lord of your life. Philippians 2:10-11

   Intellectual conclusions or emotional responses are not the same as saving faith.

   Question: Can you recall times when you mistook an accepted idea about God or Jesus as the same as faith? How was saving faith different?

4. **We were turned.** 1 Thessalonians 1:9
   Conversion simply means to be turned. In conversion, your heart, mind, emotion, will, personality, and physical energy turn to God. Mark 10:17-22

   Moral reformation is not the same thing as conversion. Reformation often focuses on our *works of righteousness* and usually involves some form of bargaining where we offer something to God in exchange for something in return, such as peace of mind or a chance at heaven. Conversion takes place deep in our hearts and is not an act of bargaining with God; it is an act of *willing surrender* to Him that presents itself in *ready obedience* to Him.

Question: Can you recall resolutions or moral pledges you have made to God in the past instead of turning your life to Christ? What did you try to do, and how long did it last? What were some of the immediate responses you gave to God once you came to Christ?

NOTES

5. **We were regenerated.** 2 Corinthians 5:17
   Regeneration is when God puts His life in you and makes you born again (Galatians 2:20, John 3:3). The book of 1 John teaches that this new life will produce an evident change in the Christian.

   o   You do not continue in the same pattern of sin. 1 John 2:3-6
   o   You love God and not the world. 1 John 2:9–11, 15–17
   o   God gives you a mind to understand truth. 1 John 2:25-27

   Regeneration is not just getting religious. It is not a life of trying harder. It is an internal transformation of God making you what you could not be without Him.

   Question: Can you recall times when you practiced some religion but did not live a life of regeneration or in relationship with God? Describe the religious life you practiced that did not display regeneration. What are some of the character traits of God that He has put into you since He brought you to saving faith?

6. **We received the witness of the Spirit.** Romans 8:13-16
   The witness of the Spirit is a confirmation, from God, that you are a true believer. The witness of the Spirit sounds within you in the face of trials and temptations.

   Jesus said that in the end many will stand before Him crying "Lord, Lord!" with false assurances of salvation. Assurances such as these are usually based on a false confidence in acts of moral reformation, intellectual assent, or emotional response. These may instead be expressions of God *preparing* grace in your life, *but not saving grace.*

NOTES

Question: Can you think of assurances that you once claimed for a saving faith that did nothing to prevent you from wandering away from God? Give some examples of false assurances you once claimed.

Question: Having repented and believed in Jesus as your Savior, in what way did you enter into a battle against sin and temptation that you had not known before? How did you call out to God and find that He helped you in this new fight to be holy?

> We must make sure, for our own sake and for the sake of our witness, that our personal testimonies cannot be duplicated by those who do not follow Christ. We must make sure that our testimonies point to a saving encounter with the living Christ and are not simply testimonies to a cultural Christianity.

ASSIGNMENT

- Write out your own testimony of salvation following the outline that Paul used.
- Make sure that your testimony includes the six essential experiences of salvation.

~

"I am an intercessor. I represent God to people and people to God. Therefore, I must take time to know God and take time to know people. I know that the Holy Spirit works ahead of me speaking into the lives of unbelievers. I want to join that conversation by listening to them and then telling them the good news."

5

Now when they heard this they were cut to the heart, and said to Peter and the rest of the apostles, "Brothers, what shall we do?"

Acts 2:37

Step 5: Discover What People Know About God and About Their Sin

REVIEW OF STEP 4
We learned that a genuine personal testimony of salvation often triggers responses of both rejection and persuasion. Like Festus, an unbelieving person might think that the one sharing that testimony is crazy. And yet, like Agrippa, that person might also sense its persuasion. We learned Paul's outline in sharing his testimony: his life before coming to Christ, the events that brought him to Christ, how he turned to Christ, and finally, his life since following Christ. We also learned the six essential experiences found in the story of personal salvation: awakening, repentance, saving faith, conversion or turning, regeneration, and receiving the witness of the Holy Spirit.

LAST WEEK'S ASSIGNMENT
Participants will spend time as a class or in smaller groups sharing with each other their testimony of salvation. Those listening should determine if the testimony being shared follows Paul's basic outline as well as if it includes the six essential experiences of personal salvation. After each person shares, the group should discuss the person's testimony to affirm it or, if necessary, to challenge it.

INTRODUCTION TO STEP 5
After a period of dedicated Intercession for the lost people in our *oikos,* there is a need to move intentionally into gracious dialogue with each person. This will be a conversation where we listen for the evidence of God's preparing grace and we share the message of God's saving grace. Now that we are armed with the gospel and the story of our own salvation, we are compelled by Christ to actively pursue opportunities to speak of these things with lost people.

LEARNING OBJECTIVES
We will learn how to start a dialogue using questions that will help people share what God is revealing to them about Himself. We will learn to trust the Holy Spirit to make those with whom we dialogue more aware of their sins and help them see their need before God.

STARTING A DIALOGUE

We have been praying for our friends for some time now. They know this. It is time to contact them and arrange a visit for a serious conversation. How should we arrange this?

1. **Be direct with your intentions.**

   - Remind them that you have been faithfully praying for them.
   - Let them know that you want to talk about how God has worked in your own life.
   - Set up a specific place and time to visit; at their home; for lunch, tea, coffee; etc.

2. **Use your own story.** They have agreed to meet with you, and you are sitting with them. Now what should you do?

   - After a time of talking, transition by restating the reason for your visit.
   - Then share your own spiritual journey and conversion to Christ, making sure you do not speak too long.
   - Consider using a written testimony so you can be concise and so you do not forget the central elements.
   - Make use of your testimony during the conversation, remembering your own condition and struggles.

3. **Use dialogue questions to reveal the gospel.**

   - Move to asking dialogue questions that explore the convicting work of the Holy Spirit in their life.
   - "I really want to know what you believe about these things. Can I ask you some questions?"
   - Make sure you are ready to listen.

HAVE A PLAN

The following outline is not a script or a formula. It is a map. It will trace the topics of dialogue that we should pursue with an unbeliever following a period of committed intercession. Use the following questions and subsequent dialogue questions as a guide to help you move the conversation forward meaningfully. Following each question is a suggested verse.

NOTES

We recommend you consider sharing this verse only after you have asked the dialogue question and listened to their responses.

Note that the first question can be answered with a "yes" or a "no." The key strategy in any meaningful dialogue is to not settle with just the "yes" or "no" answer. To earnestly seek for evidence of the Holy Spirit's conviction in the life of the person you are speaking with, you must learn to follow up their simple answers with deeper, more probing, open-ended follow-up questions. Only then are you having a real conversation. The ability to carry out this kind of dialogue is found in learning how to say, *"Tell me more."*

Each time you consider a new question and dialogue question below, take the time in between to answer the following?

- How might others answer this question?
- How have I answered this question in the past, especially before coming to Christ?
- How would I answer this question now?
- What scriptures could I share that would support my answers?

BEFORE GOD AND BEFORE THEIR SIN

1. **Do you believe in a higher power? Do you believe in God?** Deuteronomy 10:17–18

   Dialogue questions: *What is your understanding about God? How would you explain God to someone who has no understanding of what He is like?*

   - Affirm any of their answers that agree with God's Word.
   - Place emphasis on certain attributes of God, while remembering not to speak too long.
   - God is the Creator (Genesis 1:1), God is holy, God is all-powerful, God is just, God is love, etc.
   - God made us in His image so that we may know Him. Genesis 1:27

NOTES

> Analogy: A dog does not know his master and a master does not know his dog, because they are not made in the same image. But a dog can know a dog, and a man can know another man, because they are made in the same image. We can know God (no other creature can) because only we are made in God's image. God made us to know Him.

*If the person answers "No" to this question, you might say, *"I am sure there have been times when you thought that maybe there is a God. What was happening to you then, and what thoughts of God did you have at that time?"*

2. **Do you believe that God loves you?** John 3:16

   Dialogue questions: *How do you know? What leads you to believe God loves you? Was there a time when you particularly thought, "God loves me"? What was happening to you then?*

   o Be sure to probe for specific examples in their life when they sensed God's love for them.
   o Be ready to provide examples from your own life.
   o Remind them that God loved us so much that He sent His Son to our rescue.
   o Transition by saying, "Let us talk about Him."

3. **Do you have an understanding of who Jesus is?**
   Matthew 16:15-16, John 1:1–2

   Dialogue questions: *What are your thoughts about Jesus Christ? Who do you think He is?*

   Affirm any accurate responses (prophet, teacher, good person, showed us a right way to live, etc.) and share with them that you believe Jesus was more than just a man, but that *He is the Son of God.* Explain what you believe by that by briefly using some of the following suggestions.

NOTES

- John 1:1–2, and 14 says that Jesus is Himself God, and through Him all things were created.
- Jesus claimed the name reserved only for God in John 8:58, "Before Abraham was, *I am!*"
- Jesus was morally perfect as described in Hebrews 4:15 and 1 Peter 2:22.
- Review some of Jesus' miracles.
- Jesus boasted about having authority over His own life and death in John 10:17–18.
- Recount His resurrection. 1 Corinthians 15:1–9 gives examples of the many people who saw Him.
- John 1:29 says that Jesus was "the Lamb of God, who takes away the sin of the world!"

Ideas for transitioning to question four: you have read John 1:29 you may say, *"Let me change the direction of our questions by asking you something quite personal."*

4. **Do you believe you are a sinner?** Romans 3:10, 3:23

   Dialogue Questions: *What makes you think that you are a sinner? What do you do that particularly convinces you that you are a sinner?*

   - Be ready to inquire deeper into their experience of personal sin.
   - Be willing to share your own struggles with sin.
   - Read Romans 3:10–18.
   - Consider taking them through the last five commands of the Ten Commandments as a test of innocence or guilt before a holy God.

     Question: What sins do people in your culture consider to be the most serious? These sins may be different than those you have learned to address as a Christian.

NOTES

ASSIGNMENT

Take time to write your own answers to the following dialogue questions, as well as scriptures that support your answers.

- How would you explain God to someone who had no understanding of Him?
- Was there a time when you particularly thought, "God loves me"? What was happening to you then?

In the coming week, commit yourself to praying that those on your *oikos* list would grow in their understanding of God and become aware of His love for them. Pray that the Lord Jesus would reveal Himself to them and make them conscious of their own sin and need to be right with God.

~

"I am an intercessor. I represent God to people and people to God. Therefore, I must take time to know God and take time to know people. I know that the Holy Spirit works ahead of me speaking into the lives of unbelievers. I want to join that conversation by listening to them and then telling them the good news."

6

He said to them, "But who do you say that I am?"

Matthew 16:15

Step 6: Bring People Before the Cross and to the Door of Their Hearts

REVIEW OF STEP 5
After a dedicated period of intercession, we will contact a member of our *oikos* and invite them to engage in a conversation about God. We will remind this person that we have been talking to God about them every day and now would like a moment to talk to them about God. In our dialogue, we will briefly share our personal testimony. We will then transition to asking questions that will lead us into a Spirit-led dialogue. *Do you believe in God? What is your understanding of God? Do you believe God loves you? How have you personally experienced God's love? What is your understanding of Jesus Christ? Do you believe you are a sinner? How do you know this?* Amid these questions, we considered how to share our own understanding as supported from God's Word. This will help us to probe the convicting work of the Holy Spirit in their lives.

LAST WEEK'S ASSIGNMENT
As a class, or in smaller groups of no more than four, have students share their answers to the questions in the previous assignment and discuss how answering these questions assisted their times of intercession for their *oikos* list.

- How would you explain God to someone with no understanding of Him?
- Was there a time when you particularly thought, "God loves me"? What was happening to you then?

INTRODUCTION TO STEP 6
We are anticipating a conversation with those who have been the subject of our ongoing intercession. By the leading of the Holy Spirit the first part of our conversation will put them before God and their own sins. Now let us consider how to lead them to the cross where Christ died for them and before a door where Christ is knocking.

NOTES

LEARNING OBJECTIVES

We will once again emphasize listening and asking dialogue questions that explore the convicting work of the Holy Spirit in a person's life. We will consider four more points to make in our dialogue that will bring people to the cross of Christ and then set Christ before the door of their hearts. We will see how, through our dialogue, we can clarify the Gospel and apply it to the places where the Spirit of God is laying His conviction upon all people. We will learn the importance of bringing unbelievers to understand that they must decide to repent and believe in Christ and to turn their lives over to Him.

TO THE CROSS AND BEFORE A DOOR

Our evangelism is not complete or has not been communicated truthfully unless the person we are speaking with is left with the impression that a decision must be made. The pressing need for this decision will be revealed when a person is confronted by the cross of Christ and the nail-scarred Savior who stands at the door of their heart.

For the next two points of dialogue, again consider the following:

- How might others answer this question?
- How have I answered this question in the past, especially before coming to Christ?
- How would I answer this question now?
- What scriptures could I share that would support my answers?

5. **Why do you suppose Jesus, God's Son, died on the cross?** Romans 5:8, John 1:29

    Dialogue questions: *What was the significance of Christ's death on the cross? How do you suppose His death benefits you?*

    - Indicate that you would like to explain what the Bible means when it says Christ died for our sins.

STEPS ALONG THE PATHWAY TO THE SOUL

NOTES

- Use the illustration, "Record Book of Sin." Isaiah 59:1-2, 2 Corinthians 5:21

    Question: What other illustrations may we use to help explain the significance of Christ's death on the cross?

6. **Do you know what you must do with your sins?**

    Dialogue questions: *What is your strategy for removing sin from your life? How is it working? Are you positive that you have removed sin from the record of your life?*

- Be willing to share your own failed efforts to remove sin from your life.
- You should have the person read 1 John 1:9. "If we confess our sins, he is faithful and just to forgive us our sins and to cleanse us from all unrighteousness." Explain that confession means being completely honest with God about your condition.

    Transition to question seven by asking, *"If it were possible to know that, through Jesus Christ, all your sins had been forgiven and that you were completely clean from the past, would you want that?"*

> ***Note:** At this point we are entering a phase of the conversation where it may be more appropriate for us to proclaim the gospel message rather than spend too much time exploring open ended questions. Our questions will be more along the lines of asking if they will accept and respond to truths that have been revealed during the conversation.

Before question 7: Read Romans 6:23. *"For the wages of sin is death, but the free gift of God is eternal life in Christ Jesus our Lord."* To an unbeliever, this verse may be equally terrifying as it is wonderful. Take time to provide some explanation.

NOTES

- Explain death, and that death always means separation.
- In scripture there are three kinds of death: physical, spiritual, and eternal.
- If we physically die while we are spiritually dead, we then experience eternal death.

"This is what people earn from God for just one sin. You have admitted that you are a sinner and shared with me some of those sins that bother you. And these sins have brought on you the sentence of death. But God has a free gift that He wants to give us—a gift made possible through Christ's death and resurrection."

7. **If it were possible, would you want to know you had received the gift of eternal life through Jesus Christ?**

Dialogue question: *How does someone receive a gift?*

- You reach out and receive it.
- Your hands do not need to be clean. You cannot earn a free gift, or it would not be free.
- Jesus only asks that your hands be empty.

Before question 8: Read Revelation 3:20. Jesus says, "Behold, I stand at the door and knock. If anyone hears my voice and opens the door, I will come in to him."

- Have the person who you are speaking with read Revelation 3:20 from a Bible.
- Explain to the person the situation and review your dialogue together.

"This is the Creator God. He made you. You have sinned against Him and come under His just judgment and face His wrath. But He loves you and came to earth to save you. He died for your sins and rose again. He ascended into heaven and will come again to judge. But now He says He is standing at a door and knocking."

8. **What door is Jesus knocking at?**

    Dialogue question: *This is the most important question you will ever be asked. Today, are you ready to open the door of your heart to Jesus?*

    - Be willing to stay quiet and wait for an answer.
    - Most people will know that the door Jesus is knocking at is the door of their heart or their life.
    - This is a confession from their own mouth.
    - They know that the God who created them and died for them is asking to enter their life.

Before question 9: If the person indicates a desire to open the door of their heart to Christ, invite them to listen to the following prayer and decide if these words are the words they would like to express to God now. It is important that they listen first and agree to the surrender expressed before repeating the prayer.

> *Oh God, I know that I am unworthy without You and that I need You. Thank You that Christ died for my sins and offers me eternal life. Please forgive me of my sins and help me not to sin against You. I believe that Christ is my Savior and I receive Him into my heart. Take my life into Your hands and make it abundant and useful, in the name of the Lord Jesus Christ. Amen.*

9. **Does this prayer represent what you want to say to Christ now?**

    - Do not rush into this prayer, but test if they are ready to repent and turn to Christ in full faith.
    - Attempt to talk them out of it, explaining that this is a free gift, but God only places it in empty hands.
    - "Are you ready to turn from everything in order to take Christ as your Savior?"

NOTES

If they still respond with a genuine desire to open up their hearts to Christ, then thoughtfully, slowly, and prayerfully lead them in the prayer that you just read to them.

It may be appropriate to send them away to think about the decision before them and to tell them you will contact them in a day or two to ask if they have repented and believed in Jesus Christ.

Before question 10: After saying "amen," celebrate with them and be ready to give them encouragement from John 1:12 and 1 John 5:11-12.

10. When can we return?

- Set up a time for immediate follow-up in discipleship.
- Give the person a Bible if he does not have one and the first discipleship lesson.
- Do your best not to allow more than a couple of days to pass before you return. Newborn babes need to be nursed right out of the womb.

ASSIGNMENT

- Practice using the "record book of sin" illustration to explain what it means that Christ died for our sins.
- Take time this week to present this explanation and others you may think of to your prayer partner.

> *"I am an intercessor. I represent God to people and people to God. Therefore, I must take time to know God and take time to know people. I know that the Holy Spirit works ahead of me speaking into the lives of unbelievers. I want to join that conversation by listening to them and then telling them the good news."*

7

*And he said, "Come with me, and see my zeal for the L*ORD*."*
So he had him ride in his chariot.

2 Kings 10:16

Step 7: Disciple the New Christian

NOTES

REVIEW OF STEP 6
We learned an approach to sharing the Gospel that uses dialogue questions and requires us to listen to those with whom we speak. We considered how to guide our dialogue in order to bring people to the cross of Christ and then set Christ before the door of their hearts. We learned that in evangelism we must bring the unbeliever to understand that he must decide to repent, believe in Christ, and turn his life over to Christ.

LAST WEEK'S ASSIGNMENT
Select one person to present the "record book of sin" illustration before the class. Have the rest of the group contribute Bible verses that further illustrate this truth. Discuss other ideas that could be helpful in illustrating the meaning of Christ's death for us on the cross.

INTRODUCTION TO STEP 7
God calls us to make disciples, not lead people to make decisions. Our work is not done when people pray to receive Jesus as their savior. Now we must intentionally join our evangelism with the ongoing work of personal discipleship. The conversation that the Holy Spirit is having with each person continues after they believe in Christ as their Savior and surrender to Him as Lord. So, our role and our opportunity to join that conversation continues as well.

LEARNING OBJECTIVES
We will learn the importance of immediately discipling those who profess saving faith in Christ. We will address our common fears of discipleship. We will learn three essential rules for discipleship. We will learn the three movements we must engage in while making a disciple. And we will see that discipling individuals requires placing them in communities of faith.

THE DIALOGUES OF DISCIPLESHIP

Once a person decides to receive Christ as Savior, their discipleship should be our top priority.

- Give them the first lesson in the "Essential Truths of the Christian Life" series.
- Make sure they have a Bible and show them how to use it.
- Encourage them to ask God to confirm truth to them as they study the lesson.
- Arrange a follow-up visit for the next day or the soonest day that the person can meet.
- Ask *when*—not *if*—you may visit them to go over the discipleship lesson.

COMMON FEARS IN DISCIPLESHIP

1. **We fear testing our hope that a person has come to saving faith.**

   Many times, when we disciple a person, we discover that they have little or no enduring interest in the matters of salvation. This can be disappointing, but Jesus taught His disciples to expect that not all who respond to the gospel positively actually receive the seed of the good news with a true heart of faith. Matthew 13:18–23

   Our duty should be to disciple the person as long as they remain open to instruction. In this way, many who did not initially make sincere professions of faith may be brought to a genuine work of salvation by the Spirit of God through our diligence.

2. **We fear the sacrifice of time and effort that discipleship demands of us.** 1 Thessalonians 2:8

   It is a fact that making the commitment to disciple people means making a commitment to give yourself sacrificially to them and to God.

   - Discipleship is relational, costly, and commanded.
   - Discipleship takes time and effort and an investment of your life into the lives of others.

3. **We fear that we will be confronted with personal needs we feel unequipped to meet.**
   You should be slow to give them your wisdom for a solution to their concerns. Instead, take time away from them to seek your answers for them from the Word of God. At the same time, remember that your most significant ministry to them may not be your words but your prayers for them.

4. **We fear that our lack of knowledge of God's Word will be exposed.**
   As you disciple, you will also grow in the knowledge of God's Word. If you don't know the Bible's answer to a question, discuss seeking an answer through a prayerful study of God's Word, and suggest that the next time you meet you both share what you learned.

RULE #1: NO EVANGELISM WITHOUT DISCIPLESHIP
Read Matthew 28:18–20. One kind of undisciplined evangelism delights in sharing the Gospel and gaining professions of faith but does not seek to raise up baby Christians in Christ. We should never do evangelism if we will not be committed to making disciples.

> **Question:** What would you think of a person who had children but refused to care for them?
>
> **Question:** Can you give examples of strategies in evangelism that are taught or implemented that do not contain a real, genuine, and disciplined commitment to disciple those who indicate saving faith in Christ?

- We do not know exactly when a person is born again.
- Discipleship does not attempt to secure people in their salvation.
- Only God knows the heart, and only the Holy Spirit can regenerate the heart (John 3:7–8).
- Regeneration is the work of the Spirit. Discipleship is our work.

NOTES

- Discipleship is an act of obedience to the command of Jesus Christ.

RULE #2: DISCIPLESHIP MUST FOLLOW THE ORDER OF PRAYER, DOCTRINE, AND PRACTICE

The pattern of Paul's discipleship of new believers followed this order. We continue our intercession for them as we disciple them. We teach them good doctrine, and then direct them in how they should live.

1. **Prayer: We continue our intercession for those we disciple.**

    Our evangelism rose out of our intercession and so must our discipleship. Paul's letters often began with prayer and reveal to us that before he spoke to instruct, he prayed for those he would instruct. Paul prayed that his words would have impact. Prayer for those we disciple must go before our discipleship. Ephesians 1:15–19

    Question: What kinds of prayers should you pray over those whom you are discipling?

2. **Doctrine: We lay down the doctrines of our faith as the foundation for the practice of our faith.**

    A right understanding of God's Word will guide us into right actions. Paul's letters, after starting with prayer, laid down in the minds of new believers an understanding of the basic doctrines of the faith.

    - Paul's letters included a limited number of broad doctrinal themes.
    - We teach these themes in a simple manner to a new Christian.
    - We will go deeper and deeper into these truths as we grow in our faith.
    - There are no hidden truths reserved only for those who are more mature. All that God would have us know is for us to know from the beginning.

"The Things"—**2 Timothy 2:2:** Paul refers to the basic doctrinal themes as "the things." The following is a list of the basic doctrinal topics covered in Paul's letters.

- Justification by faith
- The nature of sin and repentance
- Forgiveness—God's and ours
- The significance of regeneration
- Doctrine of God, Christ, and the Holy Spirit
- The authority of the Bible
- The nature of the church
- Prayer in the life of the believer
- The walk of faith
- Our relationship to the law because of grace
- The sanctified life
- Spiritual warfare
- Doctrine of end times and the eternal state
- Evangelism

> **Question:** Can you think of any other broad themes found in the epistles?

3. **Practice: We turn to a consideration of Christian character and conduct.** Paul's letters began with prayer, moved into the great doctrines of the faith, and ended with careful descriptions of the character and conduct of the Christian.

   Some key passages of scripture on Christian character and conduct in the epistles are:

   - Romans 12–13
   - Galatians 5:16–6:10
   - Ephesians 4:25–6:9
   - Colossians 3:5–4:6
   - 1 Thes. 4:1–12
   - 1 Thes. 5:14–24
   - 2 Timothy 2:19–3:17
   - Hebrews 13:1–19
   - James 1–5
   - 1 Peter 2–5

As you study these passages, make sure you do not simply teach new laws and ethics. God and Jesus Christ should be central to all you learn and to every application in life.

NOTES

Below are three key questions to ask when studying these passages to help you pursue a life of liberty and power in Christ.

- **What does this verse reveal to you about what God is like?** God's directions to us are rooted in His own character. We should always ask, "Why is God asking this of us? What does this reveal to us about who God is?" Take time to gaze on Him from these passages and let Him be your *inspiration*.

- **What does this verse reveal to you about your response to God?** As we know God, we respond to God. We respond to God's commands, not just because it is commanded but because of *who* commands it and *who* He is. A right response to God may be trust, confession, forgiveness given or received, love, thanksgiving, honesty, etc. What does God ask of us, and why will it please Him?

- **How did the Lord Jesus, as God, express this truth about God? And how did He, as a man, respond obediently to this truth?** James 1:21 reveals to us that every call to proper character and conduct in the Bible is only possible if we humbly receive Christ as our power for living from day to day. There is only one Person who has ever lived the Christian life—Jesus Christ—and He wants to live that life through us. In faith, we must ask Him to live out His perfect obedience in us.

RULE #3: DISCIPLES ARE MADE IN THE COMMUNITY OF FAITH

Paul's instructions make it clear that discipleship should take place among a group of teachable and committed individuals. 2 Timothy 2:2

- A group setting provides a context in which together we learn and retain truth.
- If you are meeting with more than one new believer at a time, you should intentionally think of this group as an expression of the body of Christ gathering in community.

This group can grow as you reach out to others or as you invite others into it.
- Even if you are meeting with a new believer one-on-one, consider inviting a Christian brother or sister to join you in your time together after the first or second lesson.
- Set the goal that between the fourth and sixth lesson you will have the new believer engaged in a small group setting or attending a fellowship meeting in the local church.

HAVE A PLAN

Church Partnership Evangelism provides basic discipleship lessons developed around the truths and ideas explored above, titled, "Essential Truths of the Christian Life." The Holy Spirit is responsible for leading new believers to understand God's word. In partnership with the Spirit, a clear resource can help any Christian, new or old, to be comfortable teaching new believers in the doctrines and conducts of the Christian life.

- Your time should begin with prayer as you ask God to guide you in your study of His Word.
- At the first lesson, show the new believer how their Bible is organized. Using the table of contents, show them where to find the various books, chapters, and verses.
- Share reading different parts of the lessons with the person who you are discipling.
- As you come to verses in the lesson, allow the new believer to practice finding and reading them aloud.
- Give the person time to answer questions from the lesson and give them as little help as possible. Let them think through the questions and keep taking them back to the Bible for answers.
- Let your conversation on these lessons be simple. What is meat to you must be given as milk to them.
- Take the attitude of learning together.

NOTES

NOTES

ASSIGNMENT

- With your partner, decide that one of you will play the role of leader and the other of a new Christian, and practice going through the first lesson of "Essential Truths of the Christian Life" together.
- Be sure to show them how to use the Bible and pray with one another before and after the lesson.

~

"I am an intercessor. I represent God to people and people to God. Therefore, I must take time to know God and take time to know people. I know that the Holy Spirit works ahead of me speaking into the lives of unbelievers. I want to join that conversation by listening to them and then telling them the good news." My conversation does not end if they decide to repent and believe in the Lord Jesus; it must move immediately to making a disciple."

8

And when they had prayed, the place in which they were gathered together was shaken, and they were all filled with the Holy Spirit and continued to speak the word of God with boldness.

Acts 4:31

Step 8: Be Filled with the Holy Spirit

NOTES

REVIEW OF STEP 7
We learned that we must be committed to an immediate transition from evangelism to discipleship. We learned the three essential rules for discipleship. First, we should not evangelize without discipling those who profess faith in Christ. Second, discipleship must follow the order of prayer, doctrine, and practice. Third, disciples are made in communities of faith. Throughout our lesson, we learned practical advice on continuing this conversation of discipleship.

LAST WEEK'S ASSIGNMENT
Prayer partners were assigned the task of practicing the first discipleship lesson with one another. Discuss the benefits of your time of practice in the first lesson. What do you think are the most important truths of the Christian life to teach a new Christian? How much time and for how long do you think you must work to disciple another person, and why?

INTRODUCTION TO STEP 8
The truth is that much of what we have learned could be practiced by a Christian as an exercise of their own effort. That Christian's evangelism may look and feel like real and genuine evangelism, but it is wholly inadequate so long as is it is not compelled and propelled by the Spirit of God in them. The Holy Spirit is ready to fill us and we should not take another step in the way of evangelism without the filling of the Holy Spirit who goes with us and goes before us.

LEARNING OBJECTIVES
We will remind ourselves of how the work of the Holy Spirit affects our evangelism. We will consider the promised gift of the Holy Spirit that Jesus gave to the apostles and to us. Most importantly, we will discover the moment when the Holy Spirit fills a person and how to be filled with the Holy Spirit.

A WORK THAT DEPENDS ON THE HOLY SPIRIT

Let us remember the ongoing work of the Holy Spirit and our dependence on that work for our witness.

- The Holy Spirit convicts lost people of their sin, their need for and lack of righteousness, and because of this, the inevitability of judgment.
- The Holy Spirit has been convicting humanity since the fall (*pre*-Pentecostal).
- The Spirit's conviction climaxes in the witness of Christ from a Spirit-filled church (*post*-Pentecostal).

John 16:8–11
The coming of the Holy Spirit at Pentecost was directly connected to the convicting witness of the church.

John 15:26–27
The Holy Spirit came to bear witness of Christ to us so that we can bear witness of Christ to others.

Luke 24:46–49 and Acts 1:8
The promise of the Holy Spirit directly relates to our witness of Jesus Christ to a world of lost people.

THE FILLING OF THE HOLY SPIRIT

For the work of intercession, evangelism, and discipleship, we need God's power. The Holy Spirit is ready to fill us. We should commit to not taking another step without this filling of the Holy Spirit. The Holy Spirit fills the Christian with the *presence* and *power* of Jesus Christ *so that* we give witness to Him.

1. **Filled with presence.**

    - The Lord Jesus told the disciples that the Holy Spirit would express Jesus' own life to them so that, with the coming of the Holy Spirit, Jesus Himself would come to them. John 14:16–20
    - The Holy Spirit is the Spirit of Christ's presence. He makes the Lord Jesus real to us. Ephesians 3:17

2. **Filled with power.**

    o   The Spirit empowers our proclamation of the Gospel. 1 Thessalonians 1:5
    o   Our Lord spoke with convicting power, and we have been granted authority and power to speak in the same manner by His Spirit.
    o   The Holy Spirit is also the Spirit of Christ' power, making Christ real through us. Ephesians 3:16
    o   By the Spirit's fullness we *listen* and then we *speak*. We cannot do this without it.

MISSING OUT ON THE HOLY SPIRIT'S FILLING

If we in the church have all been filled with the Spirit as the early church was, we would have to conclude that either the Holy Spirit has been losing His power or at least that the early church was more talented and gifted than we are today. *The Holy Spirit has not lost power.* However, the presence and power of Christ is frequently missed because the church and the Christian remain unfilled.

1. **We *can* miss out on the Holy Spirit's filling.**

    o   Paul commands it in Ephesians 5:18.
    o   Paul prays for it in Ephesians 3:19.

2. **We miss out on this filling because of fear.**

    o   Satan often attempts to frighten us away from God's best by suggesting the worst.
    o   We fear what is hyper-emotional or fanatical. 2 Timothy 1:7

3. **We miss out on this filling because we presume that we already have it.**

    When a person comes to Christ, he immediately receives the Holy Spirit and comes under the Spirit's ministry and care.

    o   *Having* the Holy Spirit is different than being *filled* by the Holy Spirit.

NOTES

- All believers receive the Holy Spirit at conversion for regeneration, adoption, instruction, and sanctification.
- But there is a separate filling for boldness to bear witness. Acts 4:31

WHEN AND WHOM THE HOLY SPIRIT FILLS

The Holy Spirit fills the one who reaches the point of intended, obedient action, and feels completely inadequate for the task.

1. **The Holy Spirit fills us at the point where we are ready to proclaim Jesus to others.** Acts 4:29-31

   - Peter and John prayed, "grant that your bond-servants may speak Your word with all confidence," (Acts 4:29) to which God answered by filling them with the Holy Spirit. Acts 4:31
   - If you want to experience the filling of the Holy Spirit but have not committed to share your faith with others, then you have not reached the place where you intend to act, and God intends to fill.

2. **The Holy Spirit fills the person who, before the task, feels his complete inadequacy.** 2 Corinthians 3:4-6

   - A prerequisite for the Spirit's filling is the desperate need one feels when he knows that God's work can only be done by God's power.
   - To call people to faith in Christ as Savior, we must exercise faith in Christ to fill us with His Spirit.
   - Any feeling of personal adequacy for this work is a barrier to the filling of the Spirit that we need.

     Question: What acts of Christian service have you done because you felt adequate for it?

     Question: What acts of Christians service have you NOT done because you felt inadequate for it?

3. **The Holy Spirit fills the person who, before the task, is empty of all sin and all self-confidence.**

   - The Spirit cannot fill someone who is already full.
   - Confess any sin and confirm your intent to please God alone.
   - Have the attitude of John the Baptist who said, "He must increase, but I must decrease." John 3:30

> The question must not be, "Do you have all of the Spirit?" or "Do you have all of God?" The question should be, "Does the Spirit have all of you? Does God have all of you?"

HOW TO BE FILLED WITH THE HOLY SPIRIT

To be filled with the Holy Spirit is not a deluxe version of the Christian life, available only for the most mature. It is part of God's total plan for His people. Do we *want* the Holy Spirit's filling? Do we *need* Him? Are we empty of sin and self? If so, here is how to be filled with the Holy Spirit.

1. **We must present ourselves.** Romans 12:1–2

   - God cannot fill what we do not give to Him.
   - Offer God your body, your mind, your past, your present, and your future. All will be His.

2. **We must ask.** Luke 11:9–10
   This is not a casual request or a request for a luxury but for the necessary.

   - God could fill us without our asking, but He desires our request.
   - *We must ask out of urgency* (Luke 11:8–9). Asking expresses a sense of need, seeking expresses desire, and knocking expresses the urgency of that desire.
   - *We must ask believing that God desires to answer us* (Luke 11:13). Ask expectantly, and our good Father will fill us with the Holy Spirit.

3. **We must intend to obey!** Acts 5:32

ASSIGNMENT
- Starting one week from today, clear your calendar for two weeks from all activities that would interfere with a time of intensive evangelism among your *oikos*.
- As you empty your calendar, so empty yourself before God and begin to seek by faith His Spirit's fullness in your work of intercession and evangelism. You are nearing the ground of intended action.

> "I am an intercessor. I represent God to people and people to God. Therefore, I must take time to know God and take time to know people. I know that the Holy Spirit works ahead of me speaking into the lives of unbelievers. I want to join that conversation by listening to them and then telling them the good news. My conversation does not end if they decide to repent and believe in the Lord Jesus; it must move immediately to making a disciple. I must act on this by first being filled with the Holy Spirit."

9

"Go."

~ Jesus

Step 9: Go Dialogue with Them the Good News

NOTES

REVIEW OF STEP 8
We acknowledged that the work of evangelism will produce no eternal fruit without the filling of the Holy Spirit, by which we are granted power to be Christ's witnesses. We learned that the Holy Spirit brings to us the presence and power of the Lord Jesus. We learned why many Christians miss out on the filling of the Holy Spirit. We learned that the filling of the Holy Spirit is a gift poured out for a specific purpose; given to those who are empty of sin and self, who feel their complete inadequacy, and who have readied themselves to proclaim Jesus to others. Finally, we learned that we can be filled with the Holy Spirit if we will present ourselves to God for this work, ask Him to fill us, believe that He desires to do so, and intend to obey Him.

LAST WEEK'S ASSIGNMENT
Each participant was tasked with clearing their calendar, beginning today, for two weeks, to make time for a period of intentional evangelism among their *oikos*. At the same time, they were encouraged to empty themselves before God, seeking the Spirit's filling for their work of intercession and evangelism. Have the participants share what it was that God addressed in their lives as they sought His Spirit's filling in the past week. What treasured sins did He address? What fears did He lead them to lay before Him? Did God reveal any areas of their life that they were not allowing the Holy Spirit to have full access to? Those who are still hesitant should be challenged to take this time to make a complete surrender of all they are and have into His hands and to then, by faith, receive from God all the Spirit's fullness. If necessary, invite all to pray as the Spirit leads them.

Next, has everyone cleared their calendar for the next two weeks? Is everyone willing to go now and for the next two weeks and begin dialogues in the Gospel with those for whom they have interceded? Is there any reason that prayer partners cannot go together to these appointments? Why? Are prayer partners ready to hold each other accountable to go, even if they face rare occasions when they cannot go together?

INTRODUCTION TO STEP 9

Today we begin a two-week period of intense personal evangelism and discipleship. Our time of intercession for those in our *oikos* and our training together has brought us to this time of action. Our intercession is about to reach its climax as we present to our lost friends and family members the *ultimate intercessor*, our Lord Jesus Christ.

LEARNING OBJECTIVES

We will discuss a clear plan of action for faithfully implementing all that we have learned up to this point. We will end our time of training today by setting our first appointment with someone in our unsaved *oikos* for whom we have been praying.

GOD'S POWER DISPLAYED THROUGH WEAKNESS

1. **The Holy Spirit leads the way.**

   o He speaks to the unsaved ahead of us.
   o He speaks with final convicting power through us.
   John 16:8-11

   > **Question:** What feelings do you have when you understand that the Holy Spirit is ahead of us and with us?

2. **There is no second option.**

   o We stand at the edge of a promised land of conquest. Deuteronomy 1:20–21
   o It is an act of faithlessness if we do not go forward in our witness for Christ. Deuteronomy 1:26
   o It is natural to feel fear when we recognize the immensity of the task and our weakness. Deuteronomy 1:28
   o For this reason, we must urgently ask the Spirit to go before and to fill us. Deuteronomy 1:30-31

Question: Why do you think God chose to use a nation of newly freed slaves to destroy the Canaanites who lived in fortified cities they had occupied for centuries?

NOTES

3. **Remember that God is glorified by using what is weak to rescue people from the strength of sin and death.**

- The weakness of the cross. 1 Corinthians 1:18–25, 2 Corinthians 13:4
- The weakness of the called. 1 Corinthians 1:26–31
- The weakness of our ability to communicate. 1 Corinthians 2:1-5

Do not allow your fears to stop you. Paul felt the same way. Instead let your sense of weakness cause you to trust in God, who is all-powerful and works through trembling witnesses.

THE PLAN OF ACTION

1. **At this point, prayer partners should be seated together.**

2. **Review the dialogue questions and supporting verses.** Make sure everyone has a copy of the document titled *"Suggested Dialogue Questions"* which is included as an appendix. You may also choose to have everyone write out each of the questions from lessons five and six, the related dialogue questions in their own words, their own answers to these questions, as well as the verses to be shared.

   Take 20 to 30 minutes to briefly go over the dialogue questions one last time with all present.

3. **Review strategy and what a visit may look like, remembering the importance of thoughtful dialogue.**

- Be prepared for transitions in the conversation.
- Commit to listening intently and avoiding arguments.

- o Read scripture from a Bible as often as possible.
- o Leave them with the understanding that God is calling them to make the decision to respond to Christ's knock—the decision to repent and believe in Him.
- o This time is not to be used to visit the sick of the church or conduct pastoral visitations.
- o Arrange for follow-up with those who profess faith in Christ and encourage them to invite others whom they wish to come to Christ.

4. **Make sure everyone has one or more copies of the first discipleship lesson.**

5. **Make sure everyone has a Bible or at least a copy of the New Testament that can be given to a new believer.**

6. **Schedule appointments.** Partners will now take the next fifteen to thirty minutes to schedule an appointment by phone with one or more of the people on their *oikos* list. Also, they will plan appointments for the next two weeks between them, making sure that each member of their *oikos* will be visited for a dialogue in the gospel.

7. **Report and record each schedule.** Each team should share their two-week schedule. All schedules should be recorded and posted somewhere that everyone can see so that the group can pray over each and so that instructors can follow up on each team's progress. Instructors will make themselves available for questions and coaching throughout the next two weeks. The team is encouraged to re-gather at their normal weekly training time to report and pray on the progress of the outreach.

8. **Pray and send.** Prayer should be offered up over each team. Then they should be sent out with the plan to meet together again the following week to hear reports on their work.

ASSIGNMENT

With your prayer partner, begin visiting those on your *oikos* lists. Visit with the sole intent to enter into an evangelistic dialogue with these individuals. Your conversation should not be quick but slow and thoughtful. This should be a gracious conversation through which you present Jesus Christ as Lord and Savior of all and present them with the need to make a decision to believe in and follow Him. Next week, you will return to report on your first week of outreach.

"I am an intercessor. I represent God to people and people to God. Therefore, I must take time to know God and take time to know people. I know that the Holy Spirit works ahead of me speaking into the lives of unbelievers. I want to join that conversation by listening to them and then telling them the good news. My conversation does not end if they decide to repent and believe in the Lord Jesus; it must move immediately to making a disciple. I must act on this by first being filled with the Holy Spirit."

How then will they call on him in whom they have not believed? And how are they to believe in him of whom they have never heard? And how are they to hear without someone preaching? And how are they to preach unless they are sent? As it is written, "How beautiful are the feet of those who preach the good news!"

Romans 10:14-15

Prayer Covenant

If we want to bring people to Jesus, we must commit ourselves to interceding for them with deep and intentional prayer. This kind of prayer can only be cultivated in us by the Holy Spirit. We must commit ourselves to interceding for our lost friends, family members, neighbors, and fellow workers. *God will guide us in these prayers.* We must also be prepared for an investment of time and effort in order to reach the place of intercession.

1. **Ask God to give you burdens for the lost and passions for Him.** See Step 2.

2. **Ask God to give you opportunities to display these burdens and passions in your actions of love for others and for God.** Ask God to show to you how you can display the love of Jesus to those you are praying for. Whatever God shows you, obey him.

3. **Here is the promise we will make.** We will pledge to pray faithfully for specific friends, family members, neighbors, and workmates every day for 60 to 90 days.

Almighty God,

I know that You desire for those I know and love to come to You in faith and find salvation through Your Son Jesus Christ. I know that You long to forgive them of their sins and put in them Your eternal life. I now pledge to seek Your desire for these individuals in my prayers and actions.

I pledge for the next ____ months to pray every day, making specific requests on behalf of... (list names below)

Friends _____
Family members _____
Workmates _____
Neighbors _____

I pledge to seek Your Holy Spirit to guide me in my prayers for them. I ask that You use this time of intercession to prepare their hearts for the new life You wish to give them through Your Son.

In Jesus' name, amen. (sign your name) _____

---

4. ***IMPORTANT: Tell them you are praying for them.** Tell them about your commitment to pray for them. Tell them that you will be praying every day for a specific period of time that the Creator God would bless their life. Ask them what needs you can pray for. Now they will see themselves as someone who is being prayed for and they will see you as one who is praying for them.

Suggested Dialogue Questions

The following are suggested questions you should consider asking after each primary question of the CPE tract. See Appendix C. This will help you uncover the work of the Spirit in the life of those with whom you are conversing.

1. **Do you believe in God? Do you believe in a higher power?** Deuteronomy 10:17-18

    - "What is your understanding about God? How would you explain God to someone who had no understanding of what He is like?"
    - If their answer is "no," you may say, "I am sure there are times when you think maybe there is a God or sometime in the past you had thought that. What was happening to you then and what thoughts of God did you have at that time?"
    - After they answer, you should identify the answers that are in agreement with God's Word. Then you may place emphasis on certain attributes of God, such as:

        - God is Holy, God is all Powerful, God is Just…
        - We are made in God's image. Genesis 1:27
        - We are made in His image so that we may know Him.
        - Analogy: A dog does not know his master and a master does not know his dog, because they are not made in the same image. But a dog can know a dog, a man can know another man, because they are made in the same image. We can know God (no other creature can) because only we are made in His image. God made us to know Him.

2. **Do you believe that God loves you?** John 3:16

    - "What leads you to believe God loves you?"
    - "Is there a time when you particularly felt, 'God loves me'? What was happening to you then?"

3. **According to your understanding, who do you think Jesus is?**
    Matthew 16:15-16, John 1:1-2
    Do you believe that Jesus is the Son of God? (alternative)

    - "What are your thoughts about Jesus Christ? Who do you think that He is?"
    - "I'd like to explain to you why I believe Jesus was the Son of God and what I believe that means."

        - Review his claims. John 8:58 says, "…before Abraham was born, I am!"
        - Restate his moral perfection. Hebrews 4:15, 1 Peter 2:22, John 8:46. Jesus challenged, "Which one of you convicts me of sin?"

- Review his miracles.
- Review his boast about death. John 10:17-18 says, "No one takes my life from me [...] I have the power to lay it down and the power to take it up again."
- Recount his resurrection, noting that many saw Him. 1 Corinthians 15:1-9
- Read John 1:1-2, 14.

4. **Do you believe you are a sinner?** Romans 3:10, 3:23

   - "What makes you think that you are a sinner? What do you do that particularly convinces you that you are a sinner?"
   - Read Romans 3:10-18
   - Consider taking them through the last five commands of the Ten Commandments as a test of innocence or guilt before a holy God. Exodus 20:13-17

5. **Why do you suppose Jesus, God's Son, died on the cross?** Romans 5:8, John 1:29
   Do you believe that Jesus Christ died for your sins? (alternative)

   - "What do you think the significance was of Christ's death on the Cross?"
   - "Let me explain to you what the Bible means in telling us Christ died for our sins."
   - Use the Illustration of the "record book of sin." 2 Corinthians 5:21

6. **Do you know what you must do with your sins?**

   - "How do you think a person can get rid of their sins?"
   - "What is your strategy for removing sin from your life?"
   - "How is it working for you?"
   - "Are you positive that they are gone from the record of your life?"
   - Then read to them 1 John 1:9.

The Bible says in 1 John 1:9, *"If you confess your sins, He is faithful and just to forgive us our sins, and to cleanse us from all unrighteousness."* Do you believe this?

- Explain that *confession* means telling God the truth.
- "I'm a sinner. My sins bring upon me Your judgment. I cannot be saved from this problem unless You rescue me."
- Ask the *hypothetical* question, "If it were possible would you want to know that all your sins were forgiven through the Lord Jesus?"

Before question 7: Romans 6:23 says, *"For the wages of sin is death, but the gift of God is eternal life through Jesus Christ our Lord."*

- Explain death; that death always means separation.

    o There are three kinds of death in scripture: physical, spiritual, and eternal death.
    o If we physically die while we are spiritually dead, we will experience eternal death.

- "This is what all people have earned from God from just one sin."
- "But God has a free gift He wants to give us – a gift made possible through Christ death and resurrection."

7. **If it were possible, would you want to know you had received the gift of eternal life through Jesus Christ?**

    - Ask, "How do you receive a gift?" You reach out and receive it!
    - Your hands do not need to be clean. You cannot earn a free gift, or else it would not be free.
    - Jesus only asks that your hands be empty.

Before question 8: In Revelation 3:20 Jesus says, *"Behold, I stand at the door and knock. If anyone hears my voice and opens the door, I will come in to him."*

- Have the person you are speaking with read Revelation 3:20 from a Bible.
- Explain to the person the situation and review your dialogue together.
- "This is the Creator God. He made you. You have sinned against Him and come under His just judgment and face His wrath. But He loves you and came to earth to save you. He died for your sins and rose again. He ascended into heaven and will come again to judge. But now He says He is standing at a door and knocking."

8. **What door is Jesus knocking at?**

    - Be willing to stay quiet and wait for an answer.
    - Most people will know that Jesus is knocking at the door to their heart or their life.
    - This is a confession from their own mouth.
    - They know that the God who created them and died for them is asking to enter their life.
    - "This is the most important question you will ever be asked, **Today, are you ready to open the door of your heart to Jesus?**

Before question 9: If the person indicates a desire to open the door of their heart to Christ, invite them to listen to the following prayer and decide if these are the words that they would like to express to God now. It is important that they listen first and agree to the surrender expressed before repeating the prayer.

> Oh God, I know that I am unworthy without You and that I need You. Thank You that Christ died for my sins and offers me eternal life. Please forgive me of my sins and help me not to sin against You. I believe that Christ is my Savior and I receive Him into my heart. Take my life into Your hands and make it abundant and useful, in the name of the Lord Jesus Christ. Amen.

9. **Does this prayer represent what you want to say to Christ now?**

   - Do not rush into this prayer.
   - Test the person to see if they are ready to repent and turn to Christ in full faith.
   - Attempt to talk them out of it, explaining that this is a free gift, but God only places it in empty hands.
   - "Are you ready to turn from everything in order to take Christ as your Savior?"
   - If so, please repeat this prayer after me, phrase by phrase.

Before question 10: After saying "amen," celebrate with them and be ready to give them encouragement from John 1:12 and 1 John 5:11-12.

   - "After saying this prayer, do you believe that Christ has entered your heart, and that He has forgiven you of your sins as it says in 1 John 1:9?"
   - Do you believe now that you are a son or daughter of God as it says in John 1:12?
   - You may choose to read them 1 John 5:11-12.
   - "Do you have the Son? And if so, what else do you now have?"
   - The answer: ETERNAL LIFE!!!

10. **When can we return?**

    - Set up a time for immediate follow-up in discipleship.
    - Give the person a Bible if he does not have one and the first discipleship lesson.
    - If you can return the next day to go through the first lesson with them, do.
    - Do your best not to allow more than a couple of days to pass before you return. Newborn babes need to be nursed right out of the womb.

10 Questions

Take some notes next to these questions, then tear out this page and bring it with you as you go and converse with others about the good news. Or make it your Bible's bookmark!

You can some extra copies of this simple guide on the next page. You can also find more at: www.traincpe.org.

1. **Do you believe in God? (Deut. 10:17-18)**
   What is He like? How would you describe Him?

2. **Do you believe God loves you? (Jn. 3:16)**
   How do you know? What has He done for you?

3. **Do you know who Jesus is? (Jn. 1:1-2, 14)**
   Who was He? What did He do?

4. **Do you believe you are a sinner? (Rom. 3:23, Rom. 3:10-18)**
   How do you know? What do you do that convinces you that you are a sinner?

5. **Do you believe Jesus died for your sins? (Rom. 5:8, Jn. 1:29)**
   Why did He? What do you think it means that He died for your sins?

6. **Do you know what you must do with your sins? (1 Jn. 1:9)**
   What has been your strategy for removing sin from your life? How is it working?

Before question 7: Read Rom. 6:23

7. **If it were possible, is this a gift you would want to receive?**
   How does someone receive a gift?

Before question 8: Read Rev. 3:20

8. **What door is Jesus knocking at?**
   Today, are you ready to repent and open the door of your heart to Jesus?

Before question 9: If they say yes, read this prayer:

> Oh God, I know that I am unworthy without You and that I need You. Thank You that Christ died for my sins and offers me eternal life. Please forgive me of my sins and help me not to sin against You. I believe that Christ is my Savior and I receive Him into my heart. Take my life into Your hands and make it abundant and useful, in the name of the Lord Jesus Christ. Amen.

9. **Does this prayer express what you want to say to Christ now?**

Before question 10: Celebrate! Jn. 1:12

10. **When can we get together again?**

1. **Do you believe in God?** (Deut. 10:17-18)
   What is He like? How would you describe Him?

2. **Do you believe God loves you?** (Jn. 3:16)
   How do you know? What has He done for you?

3. **Do you know who Jesus is?** (Jn. 1:1-2, 14)
   Who was He? What did He do?

4. **Do you believe you are a sinner?**
   (Rom. 3:23, Rom. 3:10-18)
   How do you know? What do you do that convinces you that you are a sinner?

5. **Do you believe Jesus died for your sins?**
   (Rom. 5:8, Jn. 1:29)
   Why did He? What do you think it means that He died for your sins?

6. **Do you know what you must do with your sins? (1 Jn. 1:9)**
   What has been your strategy for removing sin from your life? How is it working?

Before question 7: Read Rom. 6:23
7. **If it were possible, is this a gift you would want to receive?**
   How does someone receive a gift?

Before question 8: Read Rev. 3:20
8. **What door is Jesus knocking at?**
   Today, are you ready to repent and open the door of your heart to Jesus?

Before question 9: If they say yes, read this prayer:

Oh God, I know that I am unworthy without You and that I need You. Thank You that Christ died for my sins and offers me eternal life. Please forgive me of my sins and help me not to sin against You. I believe that Christ is my Savior and I receive Him into my heart. Take my life into Your hands and make it abundant and useful, in the name of the Lord Jesus Christ. Amen.

9. **Does this prayer express what you want to say to Christ now?**

Before question 10: Celebrate! Jn. 1:12
10. **When can we get together again?**

1. **Do you believe in God? (Deut. 10:17-18)**
   What is He like? How would you describe Him?

2. **Do you believe God loves you? (Jn. 3:16)**
   How do you know? What has He done for you?

3. **Do you know who Jesus is? (Jn. 1:1-2, 14)**
   Who was He? What did He do?

4. **Do you believe you are a sinner?
   (Rom. 3:23, Rom. 3:10-18)**
   How do you know? What do you do that convinces you that you are a sinner?

5. **Do you believe Jesus died for your sins?
   (Rom. 5:8, Jn. 1:29)**
   Why did He? What do you think it means that He died for your sins?

6. **Do you know what you must do with your sins? (1 Jn. 1:9)**
   What has been your strategy for removing sin from your life? How is it working?

Before question 7: Read Rom. 6:23
7. **If it were possible, is this a gift you would want to receive?**
   How does someone receive a gift?

Before question 8: Read Rev. 3:20
8. **What door is Jesus knocking at?**
   Today, are you ready to repent and open the door of your heart to Jesus?

Before question 9: If they say yes, read this prayer:

Oh God, I know that I am unworthy without You and that I need You. Thank You that Christ died for my sins and offers me eternal life. Please forgive me of my sins and help me not to sin against You. I believe that Christ is my Savior and I receive Him into my heart. Take my life into Your hands and make it abundant and useful, in the name of the Lord Jesus Christ. Amen.

9. **Does this prayer express what you want to say to Christ now?**

Before question 10: Celebrate! Jn. 1:12
10. **When can we get together again?**

Made in the USA
Middletown, DE
21 October 2023

41101068R00056